NELL HILL'S

Feather YOUR Nest

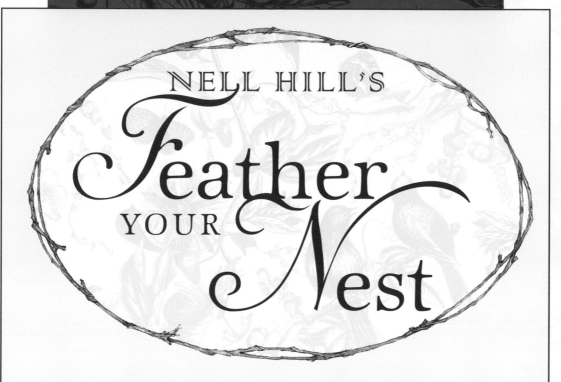

NELL HILL'S
Feather
YOUR Nest

IT'S ALL IN THE DETAILS

Mary Carol Garrity

With Jean Lowe

Written by Micki Chestnut
Photography by Bryan E. McCay

**Andrews McMeel
Publishing, LLC**
Kansas City

Developed by Jean Lowe,
River House Media, Inc., Leawood, Kansas

STYLISTS
Kerri Wagner, Cheryl Owens, Angela Stuebs, and Judy Green

NELL HILL'S
Feather YOUR *Nest*

07 08 09 10 11 WKT 10 9 8 7 6 5 4 3 2 1
ISBN-13: 987-0-7407-6858-3
ISBN-10: 0-7407-6858-1

Library of Congress Control Number 2007924703
Book design by Diane Marsh

ATTENTION: SCHOOLS AND BUSINESSES
Andrews McMeel books are available at quantity discounts with bulk
purchase for educational, business, or sales promotional use. For infor-
mation write Andrews McMeel Publishing, LLC, 4520 Main Street,
Kansas City, Missouri 64111.

To my girlfriends
who continue
to *amaze* me.
Thanks so much
for your support.

Contents

❧

Introduction

THE OLDER I GET, the more I am amazed by the natural world. Now, let me make it clear that I am not a rugged outdoorswoman—an evening on my screened porch is about as close to nature as I get. And I didn't really become an animal lover until my husband, Dan, our daughter, Kelly, and their menagerie of pets entered my life, including Momma Kitty, the cat that decided to give birth under my bed.

But now I love the beauty and spectacle of nature. In particular, I enjoy spying on the birds that live in the canopy above my courtyard as they hunt for worms or splash in puddles. It's fun to watch them build their nests, scouting for just the right twig or tuft of grass to craft homes that are true pieces of art. In many ways, I use the same approach as I feather my own nest, a 130-year-old Greek revival fixer-upper.

Like birds, we who love interior decorating style our homes thoughtfully and carefully, detail by detail, twig by twig. We are passionate about nest-building because our homes play such a vital role in our lives.

For me, home is a sanctuary. Like most of us, I pack my days full, zooming from one thing to another. But to maintain my hurly-burly pace, I've just got to have the haven of home, the place I go to rest and reflect. The things I adore, like snapshots and family treasures, nurture me. I also tell others a world about myself through the carefully selected details that fill my home. Just take a spin around, and you'll discover who I am and what I adore.

Whether you relocate every three years or are the third generation to live in your ancestral home, you've simply got to create a dwelling that celebrates your personality, accommodates your lifestyle, and inspires you daily. Through the pages of *Feather Your Nest: It's All in the Details*, I can't wait to help you develop a decorating plan that reflects your style and brings it to life, room by room.

For the past twenty-five years, I've loved every minute I've spent talking with customers at my three home-interior stores about our shared passion for nest building. But I'm always surprised to hear shoppers confide that they feel anxious or frustrated when making decorating decisions. Some worry about breaking stodgy style commandments. Others fear making costly decorating decisions they'll later regret. They doubt their own taste, so defer far too often to the opinions of others. And far too many think of decorating as a race to the finish line, not a delightful journey to savor and enjoy.

That's why I knew I had to write *Feather Your Nest*. I wanted to help homeowners develop self-confidence and avoid pitfalls as they created a decorating blueprint to feather a nest they'll love for years to come.

Since none of us have identical homes, tastes, or lifestyles, each one of us must design a decorating plan that fits our unique needs, reflects the style of our home, and accentuates our individuality. In the next few pages, I'll show you how.

As we walk through my house, I'll tell you how I developed the Nell Hill's style and brought it to life, detail by detail. Then, I'll take you through the homes of a few friends I've had the joy to work with on their interior design. You'll see how each has tailored the Nell Hill's look to match her home, personality, and life.

Lisa is a busy mom who transformed her colonial into a dream home perfect for her growing family. Jean spent years envisioning what her ranch-style house could be. Then, when her last chick was about to leave the nest, she brought in the contractors and got to work. After carefully appointing her stately Tudor in the city, Cynthia is having a blast remaking her weekend retreat, a charming cottage in my neighborhood.

Over the years, my friends and customers have taught me so much as they describe the unique ways they make their homes irresistible. And I've had the privilege of sharing my style with thousands of visitors who tour my home through the pages of my books, magazine articles, and Nell Hill's seasonal open houses. I love to hear how my guests personalize the Nell Hill's look in homes of all shapes, sizes, and styles. Now, as you walk through my home and those of my friends, I just know you'll gain loads of practical tips you can use when feathering your own nest!

Mary Carol Garrity

CHAPTER ONE
Nest Building
BASICS

I WILL NEVER BE accused of analyzing things to death. An intuitive decision maker, I follow my gut and act on impulse. For instance, I was rushing around one morning when my dad phoned with a wild proposition: Why didn't I return to my hometown and open a shop? By the time I put on my mascara, I had decided to plunge into my new adventure, a gourmet food store that evolved into Nell Hill's.

But, there's one thing I would never do: dive into a major decorating project without a clear plan. I've consoled far too many people who invested a bundle of time and money in their interior decorating only to be disappointed with the results because they failed to plan carefully.

Whether you're building your dream home from the ground up or just giving a tired room a face-lift, you must first, discover and develop your personal style. Then, create a plan you can follow throughout your entire home. I'll show you how.

DETAILS

DEFINE YOUR STYLE

For many people, the toughest part of interior decorating is determining their design style. A lucky few find their bliss immediately, but most of us have to wait for our look to mature and unfold, like a bud opening into a rose.

With great zeal, I started hunting for my style at an early age. When the other kids were out playing kick the can, I redecorated my bedroom. And my weekly dusting chores gave me a chance to rearrange every room in the house. My mom rolled her eyes, but she let me experiment to my heart's desire.

When I was a young professional and all my friends spent their paychecks on clothes, I bought art, furniture, and home accents. After I moved back to Atchison and rented a darling bungalow poised high on the bluffs of the Missouri River, I achieved decorating Nirvana. I fluffed and feathered, making my little home feel like an English country cottage.

But it wasn't until Dan and I acquired our 130-year-old Greek revival that I finally arrived at the Nell Hill's style I'm known for today. Faced with the challenge of giving this formal home the stately dress it deserved yet meeting my need for cozy, casual comfort, I created the relaxed formal look that became my trademark.

A cornerstone of my style is creating rooms filled with a mix of traditional furnishings, knitting the dissimilar pieces together with fabric, artwork, and accents. In my own home, I covered my walls and furniture in neutral tones so they played second fiddle to bold art and tantalizing textiles in every hue imaginable.

I also love to wed refined and deliciously unrefined pieces. I get goosey over silver and bone china, but if these beauties are not paired with the untamed, rustic, and delicate treasures I find in nature, my home feels too stiff and stuffy for me. So on my mantel or coffee table, you might find a piece of sterling silver polished to a brilliant luster next to a chipped garden statue tufted with moss.

G rouping dissimilar pieces of artwork in montages that randomly spread over my walls has become a hallmark of my personal style. The collection of dark portraits that frames the entrance to my guest bath is a great contrast to the delicate display on the antique dresser below.

If you haven't yet pinpointed your design style, spend some time gathering ideas. Sit down with a mug of coffee and a stack of home decor magazines and interior decorating books. As you thumb through each publication, mark the photos that make your heart quicken. What do the pictures have in common? The color scheme? The style of furniture? The use of fabrics?

Then, get out and see how others approach interior design. When I travel, I frequently go on home tours to observe how people in different parts of the country dress their homes. Visit home furnishings stores to see the latest trends, discover which pieces stand the test of time, and analyze how designers pair furnishings with art, textiles, and accents.

Open the doors to your closet and evaluate your wardrobe. People tend to dress their homes much as they dress themselves. If you like classic, clean lines with muted colors, you may enjoy the same look in your home interior. If your clothes come in a rainbow of colors, and you adore spunky accessories, you're probably someone who needs loads of pep and pop in your decor.

Don't worry if your look doesn't fit into one of the narrowly defined design categories, like arts and crafts, French country, or Old World. Many of us have a unique style that blends the best of several different groups.

You simply must follow your own heart when defining your style. Don't just replicate the latest trend or let others talk you into a look that may not be you. The only opinion that counts for your house is yours. Stay true to your style.

Whether your look is modern, traditional, or eclectic, weave your style through every room in your home so each space flows naturally into the next. Your color palette, furnishings, art, and accents will be the threads that pull each room together.

Once you have a dominant style that carries through your entire home, feel free to mix it up a bit, adding dashes of diversity in unexpected places. Overly repetitive interiors can be downright boring, so I encourage people to add little visual surprises in each room.

For instance, if you have a traditional home but also love the clean lines of urban contemporary design, introduce some modern pieces into your decor. I peppered my walls with contemporary paintings because I love the way they look mixed in with my traditional collection.

Pick Your Palette

My friends used to joke that every time Dan traveled, I repainted a room. I'm ashamed to admit that they were right! The drive to experiment with color and see how it dramatically transformed a room was too much for me to resist. After a while, Dan begged for color stability, so I shifted my zeal to the store. Now, when the urge hits me, I repaint a gallery at Nell Hill's in a splashy new color.

Whether it's a fresh coat of paint, new curtains, or a different area rug, I'm always amazed by how a change of color gives a room new life. That's why picking a pleasing palette is such an integral part of creating an effective decorating plan. These are the tones you will work through your entire home, layer by layer, in your wall coverings, window treatments, furnishings, art, accents, and flooring.

Selecting a color palette is an intensely personal decision. Some people delight in the sophisticated serenity of a monochromatic look. Others need bold hues like they need oxygen. Some like to chill out with cool colors; others like it hot.

Most of us have a signature color palette, a group of hues we've got to have in our house to make it feel like home. For me, it can be found in my dining room in the deep, brilliant blue color I call Twilight. This color looks wonderful in the daytime when sunlight floods through the windows, and it is sublime in the dark of night, lit only by tapers.

TWIG *by* TWIG

IF YOU HAVEN'T YET FOUND A COLOR PALETTE THAT MAKES YOUR HEART THUMP, GO BACK TO THAT STACK OF DECORATING MAGAZINES AND INTERIOR DESIGN BOOKS. WHAT COLORS DOMINATE THE ROOMS YOU MOST ADMIRE? DAZZLING, BRIGHT PRIMARIES? RICH EARTH TONES? FEATHER-SOFT WHITES?

SCAN YOUR CLOTHING WARDROBE ONCE AGAIN. WHAT COLORS DO YOU SEE REPEATED OVER AND OVER AGAIN? JUST AS PEOPLE OFTEN DECORATE IN THE SAME STYLE IN WHICH THEY DRESS, THEY ALSO TEND TO LIKE THE SAME COLORS IN THEIR DECOR AS THEY DO IN THEIR WARDROBE. WITH MY AUBURN HAIR AND FAIR IRISH SKIN, I CAN'T GET ENOUGH OF FALL COLORS LIKE SAGE, RUST, CHOCOLATE, AND AMBER IN MY WARDROBE. NOT SURPRISINGLY, MY HOME IS DECORATED IN THESE SAME YUMMY TONES.

STILL DON'T KNOW WHAT COLOR PALETTE IS RIGHT FOR YOU? PICK A FAVORITE PAINTING, AN EYE-CATCHING FABRIC, AN AREA RUG, OR WINDOW TREATMENT YOU'RE DYING TO USE IN YOUR NEWLY DECORATED SPACE AND BUILD YOUR COLOR PALETTE FROM IT.

NOW YOU KNOW THE FORMULA I FOLLOW WHEN PLANNING AND DECORATING MY HOME. IT'S THE SAME ONE I USE WHEN WORKING WITH CUSTOMERS AND FRIENDS ON THEIR HOME INTERIORS. AND IT'S THE ONE I EMPLOYED WHEN HELPING THE HOMEOWNERS YOU'LL VISIT HERE. LET'S MEET THESE NEST-BUILDERS AND DISCOVER HOW THEY CREATED BEAUTIFUL HOMES THAT REFLECT THEIR PERSONAL STYLE.

DETAILS

Family-Friendly Nest

Lisa and Jon Cook had only been married six months when they bought their lovely old colonial in a popular metropolitan suburb. The house was loaded with the vintage charm of the New England colonials Lisa admired, and its close-in location was a commuter's dream.

But six years and three children later, the walls began to shrink in on the Cooks. The family longed for new-house amenities, like a gourmet eat-in kitchen, a luxurious master bedroom suite, and loads of closet space. Yet, they didn't want to give up the old-house charisma and the location that won their hearts.

So the Cooks decided to stay put and undertake a massive remodeling and expansion project. They packed up their girls and moved into a rental while construction crews remade their house into the home of their dreams.

A freelance art director, Lisa has a natural eye for design. She drew upon her professional skills to plan every detail of her home re-model, leaving nothing to chance. She scoured a mountain of decorating magazines, tearing out photos of rooms she loved. Then she filled a stack of notebooks with the photos, marking details she wanted to work into her home's interior, such as flooring, lighting, and kitchen cabinetry. To ensure the home's exterior was as wonderfully fashioned as its interior, she built a 3-D model of the new addition so she could assess its overall appearance. Lisa knew that if she thought through these important design decisions well in advance, she would have no regrets later.

Thanks to Lisa's meticulous planning and attention to detail, the new addition flows seamlessly from the original house. The home boasts all the conveniences of a brand-new build, yet retains all the historic elements that give it character, like the deep colonial windowsills Lisa just couldn't give up. Lisa's created the home of her dreams and a plan that can grow and change along with her girls.

DETAILS

Come Home for a Visit

Jean and Denny Lowe had spent years hunting for a larger home in which to raise their three grade school–age children. Then, while he was on his lunch break one day, Denny stumbled across a 1950s ranch nestled on a wooded lot by a creek.

The house wasn't much bigger than their existing Tudor, but the lot was expansive by comparison. He knew the property, which was close to the city, was loaded with possibilities and would be a smart investment. So he and Jean decided to buy the house that day. There was only one problem. Jean, who was not a fan of ranch-style homes, wasn't sure she could ever love this dated fixer-upper.

For the next fifteen years, Jean worked through the process of getting to know her new home, discovering how she wanted to use the space, thinking through which of the home's features to accent and which to downplay. She started redecorating the minute the family moved in, tearing up old flooring, removing dated drapes, and painting walls. But between pursuing a busy career in publishing and raising children, she had little excess time, energy, and funds for major renovations. When her youngest was about to leave the nest, it was finally time for the long-anticipated transformation to begin.

Jean's blueprint called for adding a new half-story addition, opening the home's chopped-up interior space, and installing large windows so she could view her beautiful gardens. Like Lisa, Jean tore out pages of magazines that depicted the details she wanted in her home, like the adorable bead board bookcases she knew would look great in her living room and the craftsman-style banister leading to her new upper-level office, bathroom, and bedroom.

Now Jean's home is a restful oasis, perfect for two empty nesters yet designed to welcome her chicks when they come home for a visit.

DETAILS

Weekend Retreat

Cynthia and Tom Hoenig love to travel and adore the English countryside and its stately manor homes. So when they discovered that a 1930s Tudor in a trendy midtown neighborhood was on the market, they had to investigate. One look at the stone pelican that peered down from the front entry and it was love.

As she flipped through decorating books on the British country style, Cynthia knew she'd found the perfect look for her decidedly English home. Her overriding goal was to remake each room in a manner that showcased the marvelous collection of furnishings, art, and dishware she acquired from antique stores and local flea markets.

Through the years, Cynthia painstakingly redecorated her English beauty one room at a time. She spent countless hours stripping wallpaper, patching damaged walls, and painting rooms, until she'd brought her diamond in the rough back to its original glory.

Once her Tudor looked fabulous, Cynthia itched for a new project. So when the Hoenigs toyed with finding a vacation home in New England or Florida, Cynthia had a crazy thought. Why not get a cottage in Atchison, Kansas, just an hour's drive from home? The couple already spent a great deal of time in Atchison, attending events at Tom's alma mater, Benedictine College. When Cynthia discovered a darling cottage in my neighborhood, she lost her heart. She couldn't wait to transform this historic house into a welcoming retreat where she and Tom could escape for the weekend, invite their grown sons, and entertain friends.

Cynthia set out to decorate this vacation house in a completely different style than she'd chosen for her Tudor. She wanted this little house to throw its arms around her family every time they visited, so she opted for a casual, comfortable cottage look that still had plenty of high style. After covering the walls in bold, earthy colors, Cynthia filled each room with cozy furnishings, fine collectibles, and aged accents.

Details That Make
a Big Difference

W HEN YOU TAKE ON A DECORATING PROJECT, I GUARANTEE YOU WILL BE DELUGED BY DOZENS OF DECISIONS. THE CHOICES YOU MAKE ON SOME OF THESE DETAILS CAN MAKE OR BREAK YOUR LOOK. HERE ARE THREE BIG CHOICES YOU NEED TO CONSIDER CAREFULLY.

Area Rugs

If you have room after room of hardwood in your home, as I did in mine, you'll get to choose a plethora of area rugs. Selecting an area rug is a lot like picking a painting: It has to speak to you. Since an area rug can cost a bundle, make sure it wraps its hands around your heart before you buy it, because you'll likely live with it for decades. Don't be in a hurry or settle for second best just to get something down on the floor

I love area rugs in a gamut of colors, shapes, and materials. So when it came time to select my flooring, I had to have a bit of everything. In my home, you'll find a willy-nilly mix of romantic floral needlepoint rugs, wool Orientals, and mats made from natural fibers like sisal. I think they all work well together.

Once you happen upon an area rug you love, make sure you get the right size. I like a border of wood showing in my rooms, so I pick rugs at least one to two feet smaller than the dimensions of the room. The experts say all your furniture should either be placed on or off the rug. Since I live to break decorating dictates, I rest the front legs of my furniture on the rug and leave the back legs off. I think the room looks cozier this way.

Analyze your room and determine both the largest and smallest sizes the rug could be to properly fit the space and seating arrangement. If you need help visualizing, map out the dimensions on the floor with masking tape.

The perfect rug will add character and charm to your room.

Lighting

For a long time after we moved into our home, Dan and I lived in the dark because we couldn't find lighting we loved. But now there are so many wonderful, affordable options in overhead and accent lighting, we have the opposite problem.

For overhead lighting, nothing beats a great chandelier. Today we have the freedom to put formal pieces in casual environments and vice versa. Be playful and hang an oversized crystal chandelier in your bathroom or a rustic antique candelabra over your dining room table.

I prefer to brighten a room with lamps rather than use the ceiling light. Instead of opting for matched lamp sets, consider using a wide assortment of lamp bases and shades to make your rooms visually interesting. Put lamps in spots they don't ordinarily go, like nestled in a bookshelf, on your kitchen counter, on a bathroom bookshelf or in a large walk-in closet.

Window Coverings

Window coverings are often one of the last details people add when decorating. But they should be among the first because they play such a key role in the overall look of a room by adding color, pattern, and drama.

I love all sorts of window coverings, from shades to shutters to blinds, and I encourage homeowners to use a variety of treatments so their windows don't look predictable and stale.

Because I knew I'd be renovating our home for years, I decided to cover our windows in painted wood shutters, which clean up easily and don't show drywall dust.

But my favorite look is a full panel drape cut long enough to puddle on the floor, then hung on a decorative rod using large rings. Right now I'm crazy about pairing formal curtain panels with inexpensive bamboo shades. These rough beauties add rugged texture and rich color to a room. If you enjoy natural fiber shades but need privacy, hang roller shades behind to pull down at night.

CHAPTER TWO
Common Spaces

THE COMMON ROOMS IN our homes have a tall order to fill. Like many of us, they must multitask with ease. On the one hand, they have to be functional. As the hub of our family's life, they've got to accommodate the hustle and bustle of daily living, whether corralling herds of children or welcoming guests. On the other hand, as the most public spaces in our homes, they must be beautiful enough to wow our company.

Because these well-loved rooms are called on to do so much, they are usually everyone's top decorating priority and, sometimes, their greatest decorating challenge. But don't fear. It is possible for you to create the most lovely and livable common rooms imaginable. I've seen too many success stories in my business to doubt it.

When we entertain, I often greet guests in the entryway with cocktails and appetizers. As they mill about in the foyer, Dan and I put the finishing touches on dinner.

TWIG *by* TWIG

YOU DON'T GET A SECOND CHANCE TO CREATE A GOOD FIRST IMPRESSION. THAT'S WHY YOU NEED TO PUT CAREFUL PLANNING INTO HOW YOU DRESS YOUR ENTRYWAY. IT SETS THE MOOD FOR YOUR ENTIRE HOME, GIVING GUESTS A GLIMPSE OF THE DELIGHTS THAT AWAIT THEM INSIDE.

FIRST, FILL YOUR ENTRY WITH LOVELY FURNISHINGS. BE SURE TO PICK PIECES THAT ARE HEFTY ENOUGH FOR THE SPACE. SO OFTEN, PEOPLE MAKE THE MISTAKE OF USING SMALL-SCALED CONSOLE TABLES IN THEIR ENTRYWAY, ONLY TO HAVE THE SPINDLY PIECES SWALLOWED UP.

ONCE YOU'VE PICKED AN ENTRY TABLE, TOP IT WITH A LOVELY LAMP TO ADD WARM LIGHT TO THE SPACE. WHILE I LOVE THE IMPRESSIVE CHANDELIER IN MY FOYER, I PREFER TO BRIGHTEN THE ENTRY WITH SOFT LAMPLIGHT SO THE EXPANSIVE AREA FEELS MORE INTIMATE. NEXT TO THE LAMP, BUILD A BEAUTIFUL TABLETOP TABLEAU TO WELCOME GUESTS, CHANGING IT EACH SEASON.

SO MANY HOMEOWNERS NOW ASK ME FOR TIPS ON HOW TO DECORATE THE SHELF LEDGES IN THEIR TWO-STORY ENTRIES. MY ADVICE IS SIMPLE: THINK BIG. SMALL ITEMS GET LOST IN THESE LOFTY SPOTS, SO FILL THE SPACE WITH SUBSTANTIVE ACCENTS, LIKE A LARGE PAINTING, OVERSIZED VASES OR URNS, OR BEAUTIFUL STATUARY.

AS SOON AS DAN AND I MOVED INTO OUR HOME, I COULDN'T WAIT TO START MAKING MY MARK ON EACH ROOM. BUT OUR LARGE, TWO-STORY ENTRY PERPLEXED ME. DEFINING THIS SPACE WAS A CHALLENGE. I DECIDED TO WAIT AND SEE HOW WE MADE USE OF THE FOYER DAY TO DAY BEFORE I DEVELOPED A DECORATING PLAN. BEFORE LONG, WE THOUGHT OF MILLIONS OF USES FOR OUR FOYER.

After you pass through the dramatic vestibule of Cynthia's grand home in the city, you aren't disappointed by how she's appointed the magnificent entry. She's stayed true to her home's classic Tudor architecture, while also adding her own touches. Cynthia wanted the look of marble tile in the entry, but as the owner of two large dogs, she needed practical, easy-to-clean flooring. She managed to meet both goals through the rich vinyl she selected. To keep her entry from feeling too stuffy, Cynthia placed a large garden statue on the landing of her staircase, bringing a touch of rustic elegance to this soothing scene.

CYNTHIA'S COUNTRY COTTAGE IS QUITE DIFFERENT FROM HER CITY HOME, SO HER APPROACH WHEN DECORATING ITS ENTRYWAY NEEDED TO BE DIFFERENT, TOO. GUESTS QUICKLY PASS THROUGH THIS SMALL VESTIBULE ON THEIR WAY TO THE LIVING ROOM, BUT CYNTHIA MADE THEIR SHORT STAY A MEMORABLE ONE.

ACCENTUATING THE MOST BEAUTIFUL FEATURES AND ARCHITECTURAL DETAILS IN YOUR HOME SHOULD BE A KEY COMPONENT OF YOUR REDECORATING PLAN. TO CALL ATTENTION TO THE ORIGINAL MOLDING, CHARMING WINDOWS, AND TALL DOORWAYS THAT DREW HER TO THIS COTTAGE, CYNTHIA DECIDED TO PAINT HER ENTRY GOOSEBERRY GREEN. THE HISTORIC DETAILS THAT MAKE HER ARTS AND CRAFTS HOME SO SPECIAL WERE CRAFTED OVER A HUNDRED YEARS AGO BY THE SAME ARTISANS WHO BUILT MY HOME.

When the Cooks sat with their architect to draw up plans for their new addition, they knew the original home needed some tweaking, too. At the top of their list was refashioning the home's entry. Before the remodel, the stairway extended nearly to the front door, leaving little room for guests to comfortably enter the house. The problematic stairway was also very narrow and divided at the top, taking up space Lisa would have preferred to use in other ways.

Construction crews pushed the stairway back and made it wide enough to accommodate a troop of little girls. Then they added the historic newel post Lisa found on a Web site that specializes in architectural elements salvaged from historic homes. The wall is covered in the most delightful grid of old bird prints.

JEAN WANTED TO GIVE HER HOME'S SMALL, DARK ENTRY A LITTLE VINTAGE CHARM BY ADDING A FEW ARCHITECTURAL DETAILS THE HOME LACKED. SHE INSTALLED DEEP CROWN MOLDING AND HAD THE STAIRCASE AND BANISTER CUSTOM-BUILT SO THE VESTIBULE RESEMBLED A '30S TOWN HOME. NOW THE FOYER IS LARGE AND BRIGHT, GIVING GUESTS THE PERFECT PRELUDE TO HER HOME. VISITORS TAKE A SPIN THROUGH A COTTAGE GARDEN ON THEIR WAY TO THE CHARMING FRONT DOOR FILLED WITH WINDOWS. TO CARRY ON HER COUNTRY GARDEN LOOK, JEAN PLACED A DARLING TWIG TABLE IN THE ENTRY, RIGHT NEXT TO THE DOOR, THEN FILLED IT WITH TREASURES FROM THE NATURAL WORLD.

Foyers

The coffee table that holds the elaborate tea service, with china given to me on my fiftieth birthday by my friend Ann, isn't really a table at all, but a black lacquered trunk painted in an Asian motif.

LIVING ROOMS

When Dan and I moved into our fixer-upper, otherwise known as the neighborhood White Elephant because it needed so much TLC, I wanted to transform every single room overnight. But when the realities of time and budget forced me to pick just one area to make over, I selected the living room so I'd have a place to entertain while we were still tearing up the rest of the house. I was content to live in construction chaos if I had this one beautiful place to retreat.

Redecorating the living room was like going to my senior prom. I had more fun thinking about and planning for the event than I did actually doing it. After considering every look conceivable, I finally decided on a neutral color palette for the walls and furnishings. I painted the room Sugar Cookie and upholstered my furniture in creamy white so they would serve as blank canvases, accommodating a host of hues brought in through accents like pillows, art, and accessories.

As you approach decorating your living room, think about the many ways you'll want to use this all-important space. Is this the spot where your family will watch TV, read, or play games? Do you want it to be a place you can entertain large groups?

I knew my living room's chief responsibility would be entertaining. With its high ceilings and long, rectangular floor plan, it could easily become a cold, formal room—the last thing I wanted. So I decided to divide it into two separate areas. To define the two spaces, I placed a round table at the opening of the room. Guests could turn to the right and enjoy a cozy seating arrangement tucked in by my front windows. The wooden statue Dan brought back from Germany adds charm to my living room seating area. I added a dark screen to make this bright space feel more secluded, then filled the settee with a bold mix of fabrics in traditional and contemporary textiles. Or they could turn to the left, to a larger, more formal grouping gathered around my fireplace.

Even with young children, you can have common areas that are both family-friendly and full of sophisticated style. Lisa pulled it off brilliantly in her sunny great room. The room's cheery yellow walls make this south-facing room all the brighter and warmer. Her bold paint choice is perfect with her richly textured furnishings and colorful apple-green accents.

A romantic at heart, Lisa's goal when decorating her home was to surround herself with things she loved. She adores a look with a sense of history, filled with layer upon layer of rich patterns and textures. I adore the hunting trophies on her walls—antlers and deer heads that give her home the look of an English manor. Yet, she adds beautiful treasures like transferware plates and toile wall coverings and textiles, so the rooms aren't too masculine.

As she looked for furnishings for her home, Lisa zeroed in on pieces loaded with character, yet sturdy enough to hold up under kids. She made sure her great room had lots of elbow room and comfortable seating so her girls could flop on the sofa and do their homework or play games. She also enlarged the doorway from the great room to the kitchen to accommodate family traffic and allow her to keep an eye on the girls while she worked in the kitchen—little details that make a big difference in daily life when raising a family.

The Cooks love to watch TV and nearly every room in the house is outfitted with a set. In Lisa's great room, the TV is incorporated into a custom built-in bookcase that covers the wall opposite the fireplace. Lisa positioned her seating in the center, so just by turning their heads, the family can enjoy a show or a crackling fire in the fireplace.

Lisa added Old World charm through antique furnishings, like the federal dresser that fills the corner at the opposite end of the great room. The mirror over the dresser reflects the light from the front windows and lends colonial charm to the room's furnishings. Lisa uses the top of the dresser for seasonal vignettes so they are far from the reach of little ones.

A rustic bamboo bookcase brightens the opposite corner of the room. This intriguing piece offers Lisa yet another spot to showcase her favorite books and collectibles.

In June with Nature

As Jean sat in her ranch, envisioning what it could be, her chief aim was to bring the outside in. She wanted scads of windows that opened the back of her home to her garden and the creek beyond. When the construction crew removed unnecessary interior walls and installed a bank of picture windows and French doors, the stage was set.

Even though she's spent her career in lifestyle publishing, photographing and writing about homes dressed in vastly different styles, it wasn't until Jean embarked on her redesign project that she had the chance to hone a look that was distinctly hers.

Jean was lucky enough to inherit a host of furniture from her family. But she worried because the dissimilar styles and different wood tones of her furnishings didn't match. I assured her that she couldn't have planned it any better. I love rooms that evolve over time, filled with mismatched pieces.

When selecting her color palette, Jean painted her walls a luscious golden khaki color called Sweet Corn. I could tell Jean was a "red" person, so we worked together to find a mix of fabrics that combined the raspberry, cream, and celery tones she loved. Not only did the repetitive hues in the textiles make the room harmonious, they unified her dissimilar furnishings.

Top: *As an empty nester, except for adding a new dog, Jean was finally free to cover her sofa in a light fabric like natural linen. She decided to jazz it up a bit with a brush fringe in the same color. The center pillow, accented with fringe, repeats the raspberry tones she used throughout the room.*

Left: *I love the way Jean tucked this drum table into the corner of her living room. The soft circle shape of the table and its accessories break up the straight lines in the room.*

*F*amily is very important to Jean, and she takes every opportunity to celebrate her Irish heritage in her decorating. On a passageway connecting her living room and dining room, she displays old family photos. The casual collection of memorabilia looks smashing with the ordered symmetry of the statuary cradling hen and chick plants.

Stately *Yet* Playful

To stay true to her stately Tudor's style, Cynthia's living room in the city is very formal, the perfect stage on which to show off her wonderful assortment of furniture and accessories gathered during her travels. Because her furniture was upholstered in rich blues, reds, and yellows, Cynthia decided to paint all her walls in soft neutrals, creating an unobtrusive backdrop for the stars of the show.

Whenever Cynthia decorates a room, she invests in one fine piece, then uses her ingenuity to finish the rest of the space in a beautiful yet budget-minded manner. The dazzling Regency mirror that shines over her living room bar fills what could have been a boring corner with brilliant light. The Regency mirror was Cynthia's investment piece on this project. So to balance the budget, she set up a bar on a beautiful silver tray given to her by a friend. She topped the tray with a mix of real crystal decanters and inexpensive pieces picked up at a flea market.

Cynthia reveals her playful side in every display she creates. In this tabletop tableau, the inexpensive bust planted with a split-leaf philodendron is reminiscent of Medusa and her head of snakes. And the legs of the magnificent silver tray are shaped like human feet.

In her country cottage, Cynthia took a very different approach to her interior design. Instead of neutral walls and colorful furnishings, her cottage living room is painted Gooseberry green to accent her creamy white upholstered furniture.

Cynthia knew her cottage called for a cozy living room dominated by the kind of sofa where you can snooze away a Sunday afternoon. But to stay true to her personal style, Cynthia needed to also add an element of elegance. She's done a marvelous job of meeting both objectives. The mix of accent pillows on her sofa is both soft and sophisticated, pooling formal silks with relaxed plaids and linen florals. The dark brown alpaca blanket draped over the back breaks up the long expanse of white sofa and anchors the bank of pillows, giving a subtle yet effective cottage touch.

The large bookcase in Cynthia's cottage living room adds much-needed weight to the room and gives her the perfect spot to show off the fabulous finds she's collected through the years. A small accent light brings a warm glow to the layered display of old books, fine figurines, and decorative china.

DETAILS

DINING ROOMS

For some people, the formal dining room is superfluous. But for me, it's one of the most important rooms in the house. I live for drama in my decorating, and my dining room is my favorite place to create a show-stopping scene. I treat my dining room table much as other people do their fireplace mantel, creating an go in a very different direction than you originally thought you would. That's what happened with the well-laid plans for our dining room makeover.

Being the book-obsessed family we are, Dan and I had decided to line the walls of our dining room with bookcases. We'd once visited a home where we'd seen this done and loved the

> ## *I* LIVE FOR DRAMA IN MY DECORATING,
> ## AND MY DINING ROOM IS MY FAVORITE
> ## PLACE TO CREATE A SHOW-STOPPING SCENE.

ever-changing display of some of my favorite pieces. I want my dining room to be memorable, because this is the spot where family and friends linger for hours, sharing stories, reliving family history, and laughing until our sides hurt.

Sometimes when you develop a decorating plan for a room, you have to rethink your approach as you gather new ideas. And you must be willing to way the walls of words brought drama to the dining room. But after going on a home tour while vacationing in Key West, Florida, we did an about-face. We adored the wood paneling in the show home and decided to reproduce it in our own dining room. The paneling looked every bit as lovely in our home as we had hoped, and we've never regretted our last-minute decorating switch. It softens everything.

Country
Cottage Charm

I love to wile away the hours enjoying fine food and great company at Cynthia's country cottage. Once you're settled into her dining room, it's hard to leave. When Cynthia contemplated the palette for this room, she wanted to find a color scheme that accented the cottage's fairy-tale windows, the architectural detail that caused Cynthia to lose her heart to this darling dwelling.

She decided on earthy wood tones, and covered her walls in Molasses, a deep brown that makes anything you put with it pop. She showed a lot of courage to pair this deep brown with her living room of Gooseberry green, then add china blue as her accent color. But her gamble paid off—the room is breathtaking.

Cynthia knew a formal dining set would be all wrong for this relaxed room, so she paired a round English table with oversized wicker armchairs, dressed up with gorgeous brown toile cushions.

Cynthia has been collecting blue-and-white china for more than two decades. Instead of closing these fine English antiques off in a china hutch, she displays them on a simple butler's cart in a corner of the dining room. I can't take my eyes off this dramatic scene, with its repetition of color and variation of size.

Jean didn't like the way her formal dining room was walled off from her kitchen and living room, so when she remodeled her home, she knocked out the barriers and made her dining room a lovely gateway connecting her open kitchen to the screened porch.

Jean's mother's Queen Anne dining room set at first seemed a bit too formal for her style of casual entertaining.

I once had the same problem in my dining room, so I covered the chairs with slipcovers. We decided to try the same effect on Jean's chairs, fitting them with dreamy linen slipcovers sporting soft ruffled skirts. Amazingly enough, that simple addition turned the room into a welcoming family gathering place and instantly tied it in with the fabric plan for the adjoining living room.

Lisa turned a little-used nook between her formal dining room and eat-in kitchen into a small but stylish wet bar. Whenever guests in her dining room, eat-in kitchen, or porch need a refill, she has supplies quick at hand. By lining both sides of the walls with some of her prized plates, she livens up the area and anchors her design theme in one spot.

LOWER-LEVEL LODGES

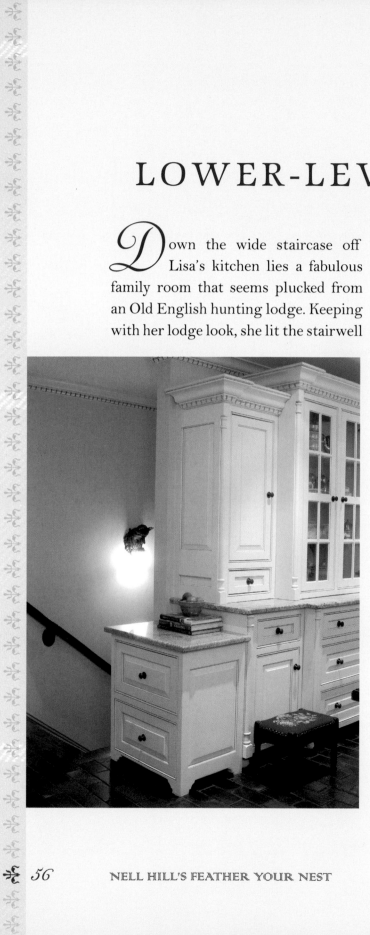

*D*own the wide staircase off Lisa's kitchen lies a fabulous family room that seems plucked from an Old English hunting lodge. Keeping with her lodge look, she lit the stairwell with a unique bronze fox-head light fixture. Instead of fighting the dark in the windowless basement room, Lisa used it to her advantage. She upholstered the comfortable furniture in yummy menswear fabrics, deep florals, and toile. Then she covered the walls, which are paneled in reclaimed knotty barn wood, with fabulous art depicting hunting scenes.

*T*ODAY'S LOWER LEVELS ARE A FAR CRY FROM THE BASEMENTS OF YESTERYEAR.

Today's lower levels are a far cry from the basements of yesteryear. With their high ceilings and luxurious finish, they are perfect spots for everything from a media room to a home gym and spa. I have to confess that I am completely jealous, because my basement is a dark and dingy dungeon packed full of mountains of stuff we don't know what to do with.

As you come down the stairs, a divine bar that's a study in contrasts greets you. The masculine distressed black wood cabinetry and mottled granite counter hold delicate silver and china treasures. Lisa picked glass shelves for her top cabinets so the recessed lighting would radiate through the entire scene.

OUTDOOR SPACES

*T*he early spring snow has barely melted when I begin to chomp at the bit to open my screened porch for the season. This shady spot is one of my favorite places to relax, with the cat sleeping on my lap and a cold drink in my hand.

*T*HIS SHADY SPOT

    IS ONE OF MY FAVORITE

    PLACES TO RELAX . . .

I'm not one for practical outdoor furnishings on my porch. Instead, I decorate this outdoor room just as I would my home's interior, with wood furniture, fabulous fabrics, and darling accents. The hutch on my porch, which holds collections of pottery, silver, and oil canvas paintings, doubles as a serving bar. Thick cushions covered in delicate cotton fabrics top the daybed. And I set the table with seasonal china so guests can enjoy a fine meal alfresco.

Rustic and *Romantic*

Jean's screened porch is in use nearly all year long. Soon after moving into her ranch, Jean added this A-line porch so her family could sit outside and enjoy the view of the woods and creek.

To make the spot shady and private, Jean put inexpensive bamboo shades in the windows, a perfect match for the wicker dining chairs she'd pulled up to her outdoor dining table. The table looks sensational covered in very unusual linens—a matelassé coverlet topped with a tasseled paisley throw.

The rough texture of the chairs and shades repeats in the bamboo serving tray on the table and the chipped painted bench that acts as a buffet. But Jean provides delicious balance by adding refined accents to this scene, like the simple glass vase holding flowers from her garden, cut crystal salt and pepper shakers, and a weathered iron compote filled with serving plates.

Cozy Comforts

When the Cooks designed the addition on the back of their home, they knew they wanted a lovely patio where their family could rest, play, and entertain nearly all year long. They decided to place this covered porch in a central spot, accessible through the eat-in kitchen, the formal dining room, and the private guest quarters.

Jon quickly coined the phrase "Friday Night Fires" and reserved the last evening of the workweek for family fun on the porch. When the weather is chilly, the Cooks roast marshmallows for s'mores in the outdoor fireplace. Lisa wanted her porch to look like it had been there for years, so she had the space built out of salvaged bricks and native limestone.

Like me, Lisa enjoys using real furniture out-of-doors. She's created a comfy seating arrangement of brown wicker, making it irresistibly comfortable with richly appointed, but durable, cushions in complementary fabrics. With the flip of a cushion, she can create an entirely new look.

Fabulous Furnishings:
The Art of a
Well-Configured Space

I BELIEVE THERE IS USUALLY ONE WAY TO CONFIGURE FURNISHINGS IN A ROOM THAT WORKS BEST. THE HARD PART IS FINDING IT.

Some people put their furniture in one arrangement, and it grows roots. They have no interest in experimenting with their furniture placement, and never add new pieces or take out others in hopes of finding that optimal flow and balance. Others constantly move their furniture, reinventing their space over and over again. I'm someplace in between. For years, I kept a large urn in a corner of my dining room, and only recently traded it for a serving cart that could be dressed up or down, depending upon the occasion.

If you would like to achieve perfection in your furniture placement, you've got to be open to change. Move your furniture around a bit, placing pieces in spots where you've never put them before. Sometimes when you move furnishings to new loca-

tions, you don't like the arrangement at first because you're not used to seeing the room that way. But once a new configuration is in place, leave it for at least twenty-four hours. You may change your mind.

When placing furniture in their common rooms, people often make the mistake of overcrowding the space. So to ensure you don't end up with a room filled with furniture, buy fewer pieces than you think the room needs. You can always add if the space appears sparse.

To get the most amount of seating possible in your common rooms, invest in pieces that can serve dual roles. Topped with a tray and a few killer accessories, a trunk can serve as a coffee table. Then, when you need extra seating, replace the tray with a cushion and use it as a bench.

D ressers and bookcases make great additions to living areas, allowing flat storage for games and coloring books, while at the same time adding height and interest to hard-to-fill corners. Tucking a favorite piece of furniture in the background can help tie a room together, especially when you have a floating seating arrangement like Lisa's.

CHAPTER THREE
Private Spaces

IN THE MAD-DASH RUSH of life, we've got to have places we can go to rest, restore, and refuel for a new day. These private sanctuaries provide us with a rare chance to relax, far from the incessant demands of the world outside.

As important as these havens are, they are often the last rooms we decorate. Sometimes, we never get to them at all. But it's essential as you create a plan to feather your nest that you pour just as much creativity and care into these all-important private rooms as you do your common rooms.

Although I love to hold public tours of my home, I've decided not to open up my second floor because this is such a private area for me. My bedroom is a refuge from the cares of life. I decorated it in vintage florals, and even though I have a compelling drive to constantly redecorate, I've never wanted to change my room. Instead, I focus my zeal on helping others create yummy bedroom designs.

67

BEDROOMS

It's hard to find bargains in to-day's antique market, but if you're in the market for a double bed, you can still find some deals. Cynthia discovered a drop-dead gorgeous double bed frame on sale, then brought out the natural tones of the wood with a wonderful blend of fabrics. She selected at least six different textiles in the same greens, browns, and reds, trimming each pillow uniquely with fun buttons, brush fringes, and contrasting cording.

I love how Cynthia pulled together a host of different furniture in her cottage bedroom. She had some of the antiques on hand, while others are convincing reproductions. I'm also crazy about how she mixed up her lighting, wedding a pharmacy lamp with a traditional bedside lamp to add movement and interest.

TWIG *by* TWIG

THE FIRST STEP TOWARD A BEAUTIFUL BEDROOM IS TO PICK FABULOUS FURNISHINGS. INSTEAD OF A MATCHING BEDROOM SET, TRY MIXING UP YOUR ROOM WITH AN ARRAY OF PIECES IN DIVERGENT STYLES, COLORS, AND TEXTURES. FEEL FREE TO COMBINE WOOD PIECES IN DIFFERENT TONES WITH FURNISHINGS MADE OF RATTAN, WICKER, AND WROUGHT IRON.

USE FURNITURE IN UNCONVENTIONAL WAYS IN YOUR BEDROOM. PUT A BEAUTIFUL PEDESTAL DRUM TABLE NEXT TO YOUR BED TO SERVE AS A NIGHTSTAND. OR, FIND A LADIES' WRITING DESK LOADED WITH DRAWERS, SHELVES, AND PIGEONHOLES, THEN DRESS IT UP WITH SNAPSHOTS, BOOKS, AND KNICKKNACKS THAT MAKE YOU SMILE.

A SMALL CHEST OF DRAWERS MAKES A WONDERFUL NIGHTSTAND FOR A MAN'S BEDSIDE. THE SMALLER TOP LEAVES PLENTY OF ROOM FOR AN ALARM CLOCK AND THE ALL-IMPORTANT TV REMOTE, WHILE THE DRAWERS PROVIDE MUCH-NEEDED STORAGE SPACE TO MAKE UP FOR THE CLOSET SPACE MEN OFTEN GIVE UP FOR THE WOMEN IN THEIR LIVES.

FOR BEDSIDE LIGHTING, INSTEAD OF USING MATCHED LAMPS, I LIKE TO PAIR DISSIMILAR LAMPS FASHIONED FROM DIFFERENT MATERIALS, LIKE GLASS, CHINA, WOOD, AND METAL.

WHEN SELECTING THE FABRIC FOR YOUR BEDDING, GET CREATIVE. MIX LAYERS OF DISSIMILAR PATTERNS IN HARMONIOUS HUES, LIKE PLAIDS, CHECKS, SOLIDS, AND FLORALS, IN TWO OR THREE COMPLEMENTARY COLORS. USE YOUR BEDDING ENSEMBLE AS AN INSPIRATION FOR YOUR WALL COLOR, WINDOW COVERINGS, ART, AND ACCENTS SO YOUR ROOM IS PLEASING TO THE EYE.

TWIG *by* TWIG

ONCE YOU'VE ZEROED IN ON YOUR LOOK, ASSEMBLE THE BUILDING BLOCKS OF A BEAUTIFULLY LAYERED BED. START WITH YOUR COVER. I LOVE USING COMFORTERS WITH DUVETS BECAUSE THEY ARE SO THICK AND INVITING, YOU JUST WANT TO DIVE IN AND TAKE A SNOOZE. IN THE SUMMER, REMOVE THE DOWN COMFORTER AND USE THE DUVET COVER AS A LIGHT-WEIGHT BLANKET. QUILTS AND COVERLETS ARE ALSO WONDERFUL OPTIONS BECAUSE THEY ARE AFFORDABLE, VERSATILE, AND ABLE TO WITHSTAND THE RIGORS OF KIDS AND PETS.

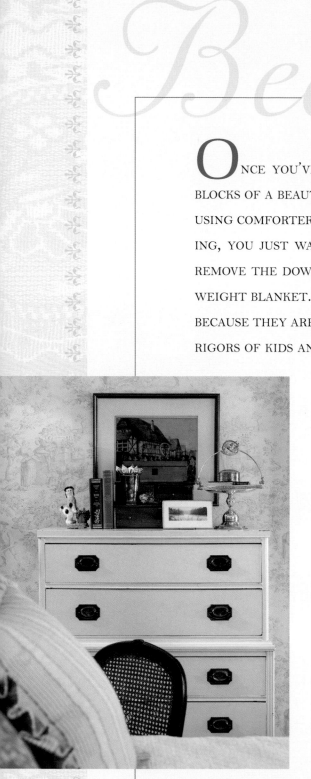

NEXT, BRING YOUR BED ALIVE WITH PILLOWS. EVERYONE HAS A DIFFERENT PILLOW QUOTIENT. I LIKE A MINIMAL NUMBER OF ACCENT PILLOWS ON MY BED BECAUSE I HATE TO HAVE PILES OF PILLOWS ALL OVER MY FLOOR AT NIGHT. MY SIMPLE PILLOW TREATMENT CONSISTS OF TWO SHAMS STACKED VERTICALLY, WITH MY SLEEPING PILLOW SANDWICHED IN BETWEEN.

BUT MANY OF MY FRIENDS DRESS UP THEIR BEDS WITH A DELIGHTFUL MEDLEY OF ACCENT PILLOWS, STARTING WITH A PAIR OF LARGE, SQUARE EUROS LEANING AGAINST THE HEADBOARD, FRONTED BY SEVERAL PAIRS OF SHAMS. NEXT COMES THE SPRINKLING OF ROUND, SQUARE, AND RECTANGULAR ACCENT PILLOWS, EACH PLAYED UP WITH ONE-OF-A-KIND EMBELLISHMENTS, LIKE BUTTONS, RIBBONS, RUFFLES, AND FRINGE.

With its soft color palette, Lisa's guest room is a soothing escape for visiting family and friends. To ensure guests have plenty of privacy, Lisa situated the room far away from the family's second-floor sleeping quarters. Early risers can slip out of the room's side door to enjoy a cup of coffee and watch the sunrise on the covered porch.

Morning Coffee

As Jean pored over her plan for her home remodel, she knew she wanted to configure the rooms on her main level in such a way that she and Denny could enjoy them every day. That's when it struck her that her daughters' childhood bedroom, located between the living room and a full bath, was ideally positioned to serve as a combined study and guest room.

Since the room would be used as a study most often, Jean created a doorway between the living room and the study to make the space open and flowing. Then she installed a French door so when guests visited, they could close off the room to create a private spot all their own. To give the room a signature look, and to continue her color palette from the attached living room, she painted the walls Heirloom Tomato.

Jean created an inviting seating arrangement under a window, where she sits and reads during the evening. When guests come, she decorates this spot with special touches to make them feel welcome, like a bouquet of fresh flowers from her garden or the makings for afternoon tea. The large picture window was salvaged from the dining room remodel. With careful planning she was able to reuse materials and achieve her goal of opening up the back of the house to the creek outside this window.

Whenever I can, I encourage customers to include a piece of black furniture like this one in their rooms I decorate to add depth to the mix of furnishings. This dark piece was the ideal spot to showcase the heirloom silver Jean salvaged minutes before her mother accidentally donated it to charity. When Jean discovered the treasures buried in the boxes earmarked for the local thrift store, she snatched them up, gave them a shine, and put them out for show.

$\mathcal{D}$ISCOVERING A CHINA CABINET IN A GUEST ROOM—WHAT A SURPRISE!

Detail by detail, Jean created a visual feast on each shelf of her hutch. Knowing that the best displays employ a multitude of heights, Jean used beautiful old books as risers to elevate small pieces, like silver-lidded jars. She also added interest layer by layer, creating striking backdrops for each tableau out of framed art, silver trays, and plates. The stunning mixture of silver and glass sets displays on fire. The beautiful pieces pop against the dark backdrop of the hutch, making Jean's guest room one of the most memorable I've seen.

Little Rosebuds

When I got my first peek at Lisa's girls' bedrooms, my heart skipped a beat. Sophisticated yet sweet, they were so gorgeous, I wanted to be a kid again and move in. As she developed a plan for her children's bedrooms, Lisa knew she wanted a look that would grow with her girls, not a faddish design they would grow tired of in a year or two.

A master at decorating, Lisa's showing her girls how to layer textiles, use artwork in inventive ways, and pull together unique furniture treasures to make a room that's harmonious and beautiful.

When it was time for three-year-old Georgia to graduate from her baby

bed, she moved up with style. Now she sleeps in a lovely French upholstered bed festooned with a garden of pillows. Lisa discovered the one-of-a-kind bed at an antique mall, but it was a bit low for her liking, so she made it taller by extending each leg, camouflaging her handiwork with a dab of paint.

Lisa fell in love with a carpet dotted with rosebuds and decided to repeat the rosebud motif in subtle ways throughout the room. Layer after layer, Lisa artfully combined a host of fabrics and trims to create one of the most beautiful beds I've ever seen. Tea-stained florals intertwine beautifully with striped taffeta and cotton prints, all in raspberry and apple green. When Lisa found some plain needlepoint pillows, she knew they could be perfect for her girls' beds, with a little help. She simply added a ruffle in a complementary fabric, taking them from so-so to sensational. Lisa also hung pictures on Georgia's double closet doors, ingeniously breaking up the expanse of white and pulling color and pattern to this little-used spot.

Since five-year-old Annabelle loves horses, Lisa has had fun scouting for equestrian accents for her room, from vintage artwork to new stuffed animals. Annabelle's regal bed is topped with a crown Lisa constructed from a small shelf draped with yards of fabric.

LISA LOVES FINDING PIECES WITH HISTORY AND IS MASTERFUL AT MIXING OLD VINTAGE STYLES WITH NEWFOUND TREASURES.

Bypassing passé kids' art, Lisa dug deep to find truly unusual pieces to adorn her daughters' walls. In Annabelle's room, two plaster cherubs salvaged from an antique store keep watch while she sleeps.

The four-poster bed, which Lisa painted and antiqued, is covered in touchable, child-friendly fabrics, like chenille stripes, pompons, and rickrack. The bed is a lovely mismatch of textiles, all pulled together by a common color scheme of pink and blue.

France fascinates Ellie, Lisa's seven-year-old daughter. So when Lisa and Ellie came up with a decorating plan for Ellie's bedroom, Ellie knew she wanted the high style and elegance of France. Antique stores and flea markets yielded fabulous discoveries. For seating, Ellie got a grand assortment of pieces her mother remade, like the settee she covered in a green-and-cream houndstooth plaid and the needlepoint chair she nestled by the gilt tapestry mirror. The walls were painted soft lavender, per Ellie's request, and covered with an array of art that ranges from transferware plates to tapestries. The large upholstered ottoman provided Lisa with another opportunity to bring lushly patterned textiles into the room. It works just as well as a table as it does a comfy seat.

BATHROOMS

Everyone has a secret spot where they do their best thinking, where their greatest ideas are born. My muse comes and whispers in my ear when I'm submerged up to my chin in a hot, steamy bath. I love to take a long soak every night before I go to bed, with nothing to distract me but the hypnotic dripping of the faucet.

Since my bathroom is so near and dear to my heart, I've taken great care when feathering this important private room. When Dan and I were deep into demolition in our whole-house redo, I recoiled at the idea of expanding any of our bathrooms, even though they were about the size of phone booths. A key element of my decorating plan was to preserve the historic nature of my home, so like it or not, tiny bathrooms were part of the package.

I did, however, give my bathrooms a face-lift with white subway tile and a fresh coat of paint. I couldn't wait to fill the virgin walls of the bathrooms with my new art acquisitions. The serious pieces elevated the look of these little spaces, making them stylish, not just functional.

To make my guest bathroom more user-friendly, I sandwiched a four-shelf bookcase between the pedestal sink and the wall to hold necessities like linens and toiletries.

I put snowy-white washcloths in a large glass apothecary jar and displayed them on the top shelf of the bookcase. I found a reproduction of an old suitcase and filled it with all the toiletries guests might need, then latched it shut and slid it onto the second shelf. I reserved the bottom two shelves for stacks of bright white bath towels. With the functional pieces in place, it was time to add beautiful accessories, like an accent lamp, candles, and a silver clock.

Next, I hung an open-backed, wall-mounted shelf above the toilet to provide more storage space. I filled unusual containers, such as silver-lidded jars, with cotton balls and Q-tips. I filled the remaining space with a host of delights, like silver cups and hand-painted plates.

If you have a huge master bathroom, your challenge will be to make the space feel cozy, not cavernous. To do so, bring in large pieces of furniture, like a bibliotheca, hutch, or bookcase, then decorate it like the shelves of your favorite spa.

Raid your china cabinet for attractive containers to add sparkle and intrigue to your display. Fill an array of apothecary jars with bath essentials like natural sea sponges, bath salts, and scented soaps. Put your makeup brushes in a silver cup, mouthwash in a crystal decanter, and hair accessories in a china candy dish. Group them all on a silver tray, using a piece of artwork as the backdrop.

To add weight and texture to your display, include stacks of beautiful towels. I'm a sucker for thick, white towels and love how they look contrasted against the dark wood of a bookcase. Find baskets that fit the height and width of your shelves, then fill them with supplies you'd rather not show off, like toilet paper or cleaning products.

Finally, warm up your big bath with accent lamps. Stick them in your bookcase, on the vanity, or on a table near your tub. If you're feeling feisty, replace your utilitarian ceiling light with a decadent chandelier.

Simple *Elegance*

The consummate traveler, Cynthia decided to appoint her guest bathroom like those she's enjoyed at fine European hotels. Picking a classic black-and-cream palette, she covered the floor with marble tiles, laid out to look like a solid marble slab.

Cynthia ingeniously re-created the expensive paneled look of a Georgian water closet on a shoestring budget. She resurfaced her plaster walls, then nailed inexpensive paneling trim pieces directly to the wall, replicating the rectangle pattern so popular in the twenties and thirties. Then she covered the wall and trim pieces in a high-quality oil-based paint, until it looked like expensive paneling.

Cynthia carried on the look of luxury in her bathroom by using a piece of real furniture for her vanity, fitted to hold her sink. To save pennies, she reused the ornate fixtures from her old sink. Instead of buying a high-cost vanity mirror, she ordered picture frames with inserted beveled mirrors. Her fingertip towels are creatively displayed in a Victorian silver basket she found at a flea market.

Garden Escape

When Jean's three children were little and shared the family's only full bath, they couldn't wait for the day when they would have the sacred space all to themselves. So when Jean developed her remodeling plan, she vowed to add two more bathrooms. The family's former bathroom became the guest bath. Now when her children come home, the new space is like a garden escape that's worth waiting in line for.

Jean painted the walls, ceiling, and trim all in Garrity Cream, then added in black accents. The bathroom is fresh and inviting, like a walk through Jean's garden. She's warmed up the slick surfaces with a luxurious shower curtain in one of my favorite black trellis fabrics. A painted black shelf allows her to create seasonal displays and show off accent pieces, like cream pitchers from her collection.

More surprises await guests in the walk-in shower, which used to be a tub. Two stools hold bath products like body butter, soaps, and luxurious towels. Guests enjoy a touch of spring through a bouquet in an ironstone pitcher.

Since her bathroom is short on space, Jean put a small hutch outside the bathroom door and filled it with extra supplies for her guests. Jean painted the inside of the hutch, which is a family heirloom, creamy white so it looks clean and fresh, the ideal backdrop for a monochromatic display of white towels, soaps, and sparkling silver pieces. She proves that even everyday items look lovely when showcased with style.

Tallyho in Toile

Iflipped when I saw the half bath off Lisa's basement family room. I share Lisa's love of bold wall coverings and rich textures, which were so artfully combined in this hunt-themed powder room. Instead of storing away her marvelous dish collection, Lisa uses her prize pieces in her

I LAUGHED OUT LOUD WHEN I SPIED THE TOWEL RACK, MADE WITH REAL ANTLERS . . .

everyday decorating. A playful Toby mug serves as a toothbrush holder and a silver basket holds bars of soap. I laughed out loud when I spied the towel rack, made from real antlers, draped with dainty, monogrammed towels.

Instead of sticking spare hand towels under the sink, Lisa incorporated them into a display in a wall-mounted antique cabinet. The montage pulls guests in as they investigate the treasures contained there, like transferware, old wooden boxes, and a miniature oil painting.

Artwork

IF THERE IS ONE DECORATING ELEMENT WITH THE POWER TO SINGLE-HANDEDLY REVOLUTIONIZE THE LOOK OF A HOUSE, IT WOULD HAVE TO BE ARTWORK. NOTHING ADDS DRAMA TO A SPACE LIKE A MASTERFUL MIX OF ART WITH ALL STYLES AND SHAPES INCLUDED.

I've long since tossed out the rules of grouping and hanging art in deference to my own haphazard style, which is sometimes random and rambling, and other times symmetrical and balanced.

In some spots, nothing works better than a regimented grid of similar pieces. For instance, I love rows of botanicals marching along in an orderly fashion. I enjoy the simplistic beauty of a grid of nine black-and-white photographs hung in neat rows of three. I also adore one massive piece of impressive art hung alone in a central spot. But I just can't seem to get enough of the topsy-turvy look of groupings that appear as if they've grown through the years, one piece at a time.

When I hang art, I mix frame styles, artistic mediums, and sizes with reckless abandon. On my walls you'll find portraits by plates, botanicals next to a collection of sugar-bowl lids, landscapes near historic maps, and antique platters close to inexpensive prints.

I urge you to toss out all the rules you've heard about hanging art. For example, don't confine yourself to hanging pieces at eye level. Instead, place artwork all the way up and down your walls, crawling over doorways and windows. Insert art in spots you'd never expect to find it, like on closet doors, above doorways, and in bookcases.

As you hang the art, always strive for balance in your room, placing heavy pieces opposite imposing furniture. Strive for a proportional mix of light and dark images, empty space, and color. Finally, don't simply focus on the room you're working in. Make sure the art looks good when viewed from adjoining rooms.

CHAPTER FOUR

Work Spaces

AS MUCH AS WE'D all like to wile away our days relaxing in the common or private spaces of our homes, eventually, we must get up and face the tasks at hand. Like it or not, we have to pay bills in the home office, tackle a mountain of dirty clothes in the laundry room, or forage in the refrigerator for something to make for dinner.

Work may be no fun, but your workrooms can be. In fact, I firmly believe in making your utilitarian spaces just as sublime as the showier spots in your home. I live by a no-closed-doors policy at my house, determined to make all my rooms so pleasant I hate to hide them. Even though function reigns supreme in our work spaces, we can still decorate these hardworking rooms so attractively that we actually look forward to getting to work. And since I don't do the cooking in my kitchen, it provides me with countless ways to decorate creatively.

KITCHENS

When we moved into our home, I knew our room-by-room renovation would be a long, slow process. Giving our alarming turquoise kitchen a face-lift topped my to-do list. But as we pulled together our decorating plan, the kitchen kept getting bumped because it was such a big-dollar project. Finally, after twelve long years of waiting, I was ready to wage war on the sea of blue, and craft my dreamed-of designer kitchen.

Unfortunately, by then Dan was weary of home makeovers. In an effort to put me off, he asked, "Why do you care what your kitchen looks like since you don't cook?" I was quick with my reply: "I don't cook in my living room either, but I care what it looks like!"

Like those in most historic homes, our kitchen is tiny. And while I wanted to update the space, adding new appliances and counters, I was also determined to remain true to the age and style of our home. I knew that to preserve the home's historic look, we had to keep the kitchen the same size.

As we developed our design plan for the kitchen, we added a host of details that ensured the space still looked its age. We put inset doors on our new cabinets, following the old style of making the doors flush with the face of the cabinet unit. We also used reproduction hinges, knobs, and cabinet pulls. And I installed bead board on several of the walls, painting it the same Garrity Cream as the cabinets.

Unlike my friends who love to cook, my priority in the kitchen was not to install miles of counter space for food preparation. So instead I used our precious square footage to build cabinets to store my voluminous collection of dishes. I love to look at these glass, china, and silver works of art.

Twig *by* Twig

When you develop your decorating plan for this hardworking room, think about how you will really use your kitchen. Is it command central, where your family gathers to catch up at the end of the day? Do guests gather here when you have parties? If you adore cooking, have you planned the proper amount of work space? How much storage will you need for food and dishware?

Once you have determined how to structure your kitchen, add the decorating details that will make it reflect your style. If your kitchen is French country, cluster together an ironstone pitcher, a soup tureen, and a silver bowl, then use a piece of killer artwork as a backdrop for the display.

Decorate the countertops with functional and beautiful containers. Store dog food in a delicate apothecary jar, put dish soap in an olive oil jar, and group spices, oils, and vinegars on a silver butler's tray.

Garden View

As Jean drew up her plan for her home remodel, she spent a great deal of time thinking about how to renovate her kitchen, which for her was the heart of the home. As a working mother balancing the demands of her career and family, Jean enjoyed unwinding at the end of a long day by cooking.

In her redesign, she increased the size of her kitchen by one third, removing walls that boxed the space in. Contractors moved the basement steps, previously accessed through the kitchen, to give her the extra space she needed to expand the room. When the kitchen designer pressed Jean to add upper cabinetry and a pantry in the spot that once held the stairs, she resisted. She knew she didn't need the storage space, since she markets almost daily in order to cook with fresh ingredients. But she did long for a bank of windows that would flood her kitchen with soft light and give her a wonderful view of her shady front yard.

Although she loved the new, larger size for her kitchen, Jean still wanted the room to be cozy. I suggested she try one of my favorite painting tricks: paint the ceiling the same color as the walls. She loved how the warm color brought the ceiling down and helped it blend with her walls.

*F*rom day one, the impractical hamburger grill the home's original builder installed near the kitchen's entrance perplexed Jean. She never used the small oven, but hated to get rid of such a unique feature. So when she renovated, she turned it into a cheery fireplace, one of the first things guests see when they enter her home.

Since she loves to cook and to garden, Jean wanted her remodeled kitchen to have ample counter space for food prep and flower arranging. She decided on rich granite tile for her countertop and subway tile for a backsplash to give the space clean elegance. She splurged on an extra-deep sink that could hold containers of flowers waiting to be arranged or hide dirty dishes that collected through the day.

Jean's kitchen countertop displays are every bit as beautiful as those in the rest of her home. She stores dog bones in a vintage-style candy jar, treats books as art on a simple white tray, and makes pastries irresistible under a

grand cloche. A sentimental soul, Jean treasures family heirlooms, like milk bottles from her father's family dairy business, and works these keepsakes into her decorating whenever she can.

Sunny Spot

Lisa knew her kitchen would be the hardest-working room in her house. All day long, kids run through on their way to play, plop down at the counter to talk with Mom, or sit at the kitchen table with a PB&J. So as she developed the roadmap for her new addition, Lisa made sure the space was expansive enough to handle a crowd. She also selected durable surfaces and reserved lots of space for storage and food preparation. Since she loves a look that appears to have evolved over time, Lisa used lots of different materials and colors in her new kitchen. In fact, when you stand by her kitchen table, you can see five different types of flooring: bluestone in the back entry, walnut bricks with mortar in the kitchen, oak hardwood in the great room, carpet on the basement steps, and brick on her patio outdoors.

Before the remodel, Lisa's red kitchen was too dingy and dark for her liking. She wanted to go lighter and brighter in the new space. So when she spied a sunny yellow paint in a display at a kitchen design store, she knew she'd found just the happy, homey color she was looking for. The kitchen's dazzling yellow palette repeats throughout many rooms on the home's first level. In the kitchen, Lisa offset the walls with painted trim, granite counters, and distressed cream cabinetry.

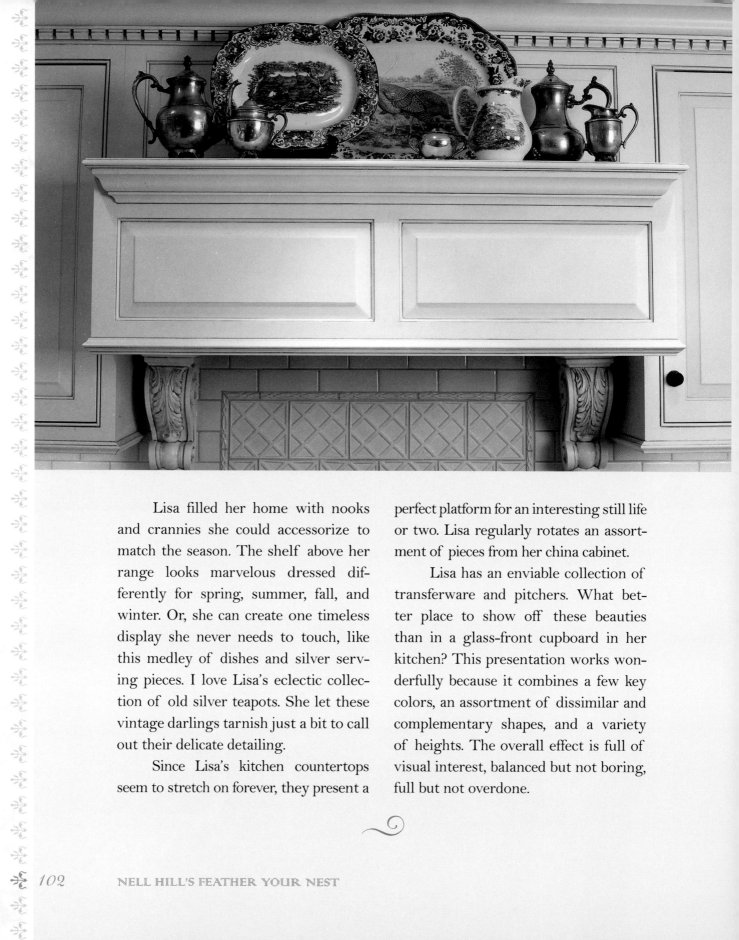

Lisa filled her home with nooks and crannies she could accessorize to match the season. The shelf above her range looks marvelous dressed differently for spring, summer, fall, and winter. Or, she can create one timeless display she never needs to touch, like this medley of dishes and silver serving pieces. I love Lisa's eclectic collection of old silver teapots. She let these vintage darlings tarnish just a bit to call out their delicate detailing.

Since Lisa's kitchen countertops seem to stretch on forever, they present a perfect platform for an interesting still life or two. Lisa regularly rotates an assortment of pieces from her china cabinet.

Lisa has an enviable collection of transferware and pitchers. What better place to show off these beauties than in a glass-front cupboard in her kitchen? This presentation works wonderfully because it combines a few key colors, an assortment of dissimilar and complementary shapes, and a variety of heights. The overall effect is full of visual interest, balanced but not boring, full but not overdone.

PRIVATE STUDIES

Everyone has those rooms where they dump the things they don't know what to do with. For me, that embarrassing eyesore was the sleeping porch off my bedroom. As I filled it to the brim with everything from donations for the charity thrift store to stacks of furniture cushions, I dreamed of how adorable this space could be.

Last year, one of my New Year's resolutions was to take back this room and make it a private sanctuary where I could finish work tasks or read a book. I hauled out all the junk, then freshened up the walls with a soft green paint trimmed with Garrity Cream. To filter out the light in this bright southeast room, I covered the windows with wood shutters.

I didn't have a lot of room in this narrow nook, so I chose my furnishings carefully. I placed a bamboo bookcase on one end of the room, next to a settee covered in white linen with salmon welting. I played up the sofa with fun pillows, including one festooned with rhinestone cocktail pins.

I placed my reproduction English desk on the opposite end of the space, right inside the door. If I was actually going to sit down and work here, I knew I had to make my desk extremely appealing. So I loaded it up with beautiful treasures, like an antique inkwell and blotter, old books, and a mirrored vanity tray covered with silver pieces. The alabaster lamp harmonizes with the luminescent hand-painted glass compote, the perfect spot for me to store my jewelry for the night.

Library

When we purchased our home, the upstairs was segmented into several smaller rooms. We wanted wide-open spaces up there, so we knocked out some walls to create an airy landing. The bedrooms and our guest bath open onto this central hallway, which revolves around the staircase.

Dan created a cozy library in this lofty space where he can retreat and enjoy a good read. The huge antique secretary to the left of the alcove is a hardworking piece, packed so full of volumes on history, poetry, and travel, that there's not an inch left over for knickknacks.

We balanced the secretary with an equally large bookcase on the right side of the room. When Dan needs to work from home, he can fold down the desk and pull up the leather wingback chair. But if he wants to sit and read, he prefers the comfy side chair and ottoman. An antique box works perfectly as a table next to this low-slung seat.

To make the spot feel more secluded, I set up an old screen given to us by Dan's mother, Mimi. For years I'd admired this unusual screen covered with Victorian prints and portraits. So when Mimi innocently asked me if I thought Dan would rather have the screen or a book for his birthday, I seized the opportunity, assuring her that Dan would definitely prefer the screen since he already had more books than the Atchison Public Library.

Top: *When Lisa worked on a plan for her new addition, she included a spacious office for her freelance art direction business. But she still couldn't resist adding this private work space in her master bedroom suite, where she could work on personal correspondence. She accented her desk with favorite treasures, like a collection of china boxes, and beautiful old books, while leaving plenty of space for her laptop.*

Right: *When Cynthia first spied the alcove off the master bedroom in her cottage, the small windows and their tarnished brass latches enchanted her. She decided to make this precious space into a private work area. Silver accents repeated in the lamp, trophy cup, and tray give the space brilliance. And the soft Oriental rug draped on the desktop adds warm luster.*

Cynthia added some fun touches to her laundry room so her pooches could dine in style. To keep their paws warm during dinner, Cynthia spread a little-used Oriental rug by the dogs' bowls. And for their viewing pleasure, she hung an ornately framed oil of a hunting hound above their bowls. You would never guess that her washer and dryer are concealed behind a black louvered wood screen.

LAUNDRY ROOMS

Doing laundry is never fun. But for me, it's a doubly dismal chore because I have to wash and dry in my damp, dark tomb of a basement. All it needs is torches and spooky organ music to be a scene from a late-night horror flick!

While I'm down with the spiders, pretreating spots, I dream of having a laundry room like Cynthia's. When Cynthia came to me for suggestions on how to make her ho-hum laundry room more inviting, she complained that the featureless cubicle seemed straight from the pages of Dickens's *Bleak House.*

In keeping with her English Tudor home, we decided to remake this bedroom-turned-utility-area into a Georgian butler's pantry. Cynthia picked a soft palette for the space, painting the walls bone white and the ceiling Amelia Blue, harkening back to the eighteenth-century custom of painting larders blue to repel flies.

Then she turned her attention to dressing up the unattractive laminate cabinets. After giving them a fresh coat of paint, Cynthia replaced the hardware with vintage glass pulls. She hired a carpenter to build a simple wall-mounted shelf, then filled it with her dazzling collection of silver and crystal, precious pieces she'd kept stored away in her china cabinet before. She's combined ultramodern accents with timeless beauties like cake plates and blue-and-white porcelain.

TWIG *by* TWIG

Whether you set up your work space in a bedroom, formal living room, kitchen, or laundry room, the key is to make it so beautiful that you look forward to spending time there, even if you are working. The first step is to organize the space so it's harmonious, not chaotic. If your work space will house a computer, phone, fax, or CD player, bundle the unsightly cords and hide them from view behind a basket, tray, or piece of art. Or, thread them through a fabric chandelier chain cover.

Next, raid your china hutch and kitchen cabinets looking for cute and creative containers to organize your supplies in an enchanting way. Sort mail or books in a silver toast caddy. Put paper clips in a china sugar bowl. Keep bills to be paid on a platter, concealed by a silver food dome. How about a snapshot from your last vacation, a petite dish filled with your favorite confections, or an inspiring piece of art displayed on an easel?

Why not give your laundry room new life with lovely fabrics? Stitch a curtain you can close to conceal your washer and dryer. If you have a utility room sink with exposed plumbing, cover it up with a sink skirt. Replace the utilitarian light fixture with a chandelier. Put a pretty lamp on the counter to add a delicate glow. Festoon your walls with great art, like oils, architectural drawings, and decorative plates.

Laundry Bliss

Lisa loves bold color, and plenty of it. So when she was faced with decorating her windowless second-floor laundry room, she knew this would be a perfect spot to add energy and excitement with whimsical wall coverings and eye-popping paint. She dressed the walls in playful wallpaper depicting a washerwoman at her work, then covered the cabinets in a bright apple green to match.

The wicker baskets with ecru liners add natural texture and soothing tones to the room while also hiding dirty duds waiting to be washed and clean laundry that needs to be folded.

You can see Lisa's personal decorating style reflected even in this functional work space. Artwork similar to what you'll find all over her home rests on her laundry room counters. And she's poked in telltale vintage accents, like twin tin-lidded jars full of mending supplies, a trio of ceramic cream pitchers, and a small accent lamp with a crackled yellow finish.

Contain Yourself

To make the work spaces of your home more appealing, you've got to keep them well organized. And to do so, you must have an army of great-looking containers.

Baskets

I cringe at the thought of keeping my house organized without the help of a bevy of baskets. I use baskets in every room in my home to hold all manner of things, from my wine collection to spare rolls of toilet paper. Use baskets to contain kitchen pantry supplies, collect magazines under your desk, or hold papers awaiting recycling.

Glass Compotes and Dishes

Instead of hiding your office supplies in your desk drawer, sort them in beautiful glass compotes and dishes. Put thumbtacks in an etched sorbet cup, pens in a champagne flute, and business cards under the lid of a glass butter dish. I keep paper clips in a large saltcellar a friend snatched up for me in an English antique shop.

Silver-Lidded Jars

I'm in love with the trappings of yesteryear, including beautiful glass jars with decorative silver lids. You can store anything in these pretty jars, from dog bones to paper clips to spare change.

Silver Cups

You can use silver cups to hold stuff in style in nearly every room in your home. My grandmother Nell Hill had a beautiful silver coronation cup she passed down to my mother, who in turn gave it to me. I use this heirloom to hold pens and pencils on my desk. In my bathroom, a silver vase contains makeup brushes. A friend of mine conscripted a mint julep cup to display disposable cups in her guest bath.

Apothecary Jars

You've just got to get some apothecary jars in an array of shapes and sizes. They are incredibly affordable and versatile, making some of the best storage containers I've ever come across. Their graceful lines please the eye, and they give everything placed within them an air of importance. In your kitchen, fill apothecary jars with coffee beans waiting to be ground. In your office let them hold rolls of stamps for your correspondence. In your laundry, fill them with spare buttons.

Cynthia made the drudgery of washing a bit more fun by storing her laundry supplies in elegant containers. Blue liquid fabric softener looks beautiful in a clear glass wine decanter with a blue rim. And powdered detergent is divine in a delicate glass canister. For fun, Cynthia decided to use inventive measuring cups, like a silver ice scoop and a silver baby's cup she found at a flea market. At eye level, she tucked some dried hydrangeas into a beautiful little china compote, making her workspace a pleasant place to be anytime of the day or night.

CHAPTER FIVE

Building Blocks

NOW, IT'S TIME TO put the icing on the cake by adding the decorating details that transform a house into a home. I can't lie to you—as much as I love the "big picture" of decorating, adding these final feathers really makes my heart flutter.

I could spend an entire day tweaking the tableaux in my home. Okay, I confess. Sometimes I do spend the entire day doing nothing but creating new displays, rediscovering forgotten treasures, and rotating my prize pieces. Not only is this feathering process incredibly therapeutic for me, the end result is a home filled with personality, warmth, and whimsy.

My culinary friends stock their pantries with key ingredients like flour, sugar, and eggs. Like them, I have collected a few basic ingredients for feathering my nest. I call these cornerstone decorating pieces my building blocks, because I use them over and over again in new and inventive ways.

Trays and Urns

One glance around my house will prove the fact that I've never met a tray I didn't like. Trays get high marks in my book because they can play myriad decorating roles with ease. Analyze almost any display in my home, and you will likely find a tray holding it all together. I rarely build a tabletop motif without using a tray as a base or a backdrop. Scan the montage of artwork that covers my walls, and you'll spot trays hung with the rest of the pieces I treasure. Take a seat at my dining room table, and you might see a tray used as a placemat at each place setting.

I use hardworking trays in quirky and creative ways in nearly every room of my house. My favorite end table isn't a table at all, but two large antique boxes topped with a large metal tray. Trays perch atop my ottomans.

Urns are one of the most affordable and versatile decorating tools known to man, and I would be lost without them. I plant my black iron fountain urns with topiaries and rosebushes each spring to add color and grandeur to my yard. For alfresco dinner parties, I wash up old urns, fill them with ice, and use them to chill wine, shrimp, or fresh fruit.

I also use urns with wild abandon in my interior decorating. Large iron urns work wonderfully as planters for large ferns, displaying a collection of walking canes, or holding firewood. I use my iron urns as Christmas tree holders to give the trees an air of importance.

Top an urn with a silver, wood, or metal tray, and you have an unusual side table. Make smaller urns work in your kitchen holding silverware, napkins, or a rosemary topiary. Use them in the guest bathroom to contain disposable razors or toothbrushes.

Dishes for Decorating and Dishes for Dining

Okay, I confess. I'm a raging dish-a-holic. I can't get enough of these fragile pieces of art, whether old or new, ornate or simple, costly or inexpensive.

You'll discover dishes in my bath holding French-milled soap, on my dressing table filled with jewelry, adorning the wall in my foyer, propped on an easel in a bookcase, and stacked under a bud vase in my living room. The only place I can't stand to see a beautiful dish is hidden away in a china cabinet.

Whether you want to create a simple, sleek look on your table or an over-the-top, showstopping display, you can achieve virtually any affect you want with a set of white dishes. These chameleons can remake themselves over and over again when paired with different accessories. If you want a table filled with whimsy, top a white dinner plate with a playful salad plate. To create high drama, surround a stack of white china with silver and crystal accents.

I go bonkers over transferware in every shape, size, and color, and I use it with wild abandon on my dinner table and when decorating my home. Transferware became popular in England in the mid-eighteenth century, but it took my home by siege a few years ago, when I fell in love with the scenic Asian and botanical patterns in blue, brown, black, and red.

I'm also nuts about majolica. This brightly colored earthenware features animal, fish, leaf, fruit, or shell shapes molded in high relief, then brought to life with vibrant glazes. Majolica adds interest, texture, and verve to any dining table.

Risers

Nothing gets my creative juices flowing more than the chance to create a display that makes people's jaws drop. It's not hard if you have one key prop: risers. These secret weapons allow me to create a variety of heights in my displays, grabbing and keeping visitors' interest as they drink in one layer after another.

You can use almost anything in your home as a riser, but concrete capitals and bent-iron plant stands are among my favorites. When I want to include serving trays on my dining room table, I pull out a host of plant stands in differing heights, then top them with beautiful platters filled with culinary delights. Concrete capitals look wonderful on my buffet, topped with a silver compote, lantern, or piece of garden statuary.

You can also turn a vase or bowl upside down to make a riser. Or, for small displays, use a wide-brimmed candlestick, with an interesting object on top.

My favorite risers are made from cake stands and compotes. I admire the delicate beauty and sturdy strength of these classic dishes and use them constantly when displaying everything from tasty appetizers to fine collectibles.

I couldn't begin to arrange a bookshelf or china cabinet without utilizing risers on almost every shelf. I'm also always in trouble at home for using books as risers in many of the displays—but what better place to use books as risers than in bookshelves.

To help your displays reach new heights, stack a series of risers on top of each other. Find cake stands or compotes of descending sizes and nest them inside each other to create a tower. Or separate each level with beautiful trays or platters.

Lanterns, Candles, and Candlesticks

Lanterns are a new addition to my list of gotta-have building blocks, but they have quickly climbed to the top of the chart. Lanterns are sinfully easy to decorate with and they pack a wallop of a punch. No matter what you do to them, they look fabulous. If you're lighting up to the idea of using lanterns, be sure to collect a wide variety of sizes and styles.

Outside, hang a lantern from your garden gate, a gazebo, or tree limb. Use a bevy of different-sized lanterns to guide guests up your walkway, or flank your front door with two huge glowing lanterns.

Inside, I reinvent my decorative lanterns for each new season. In the fall, I fill them with ripe red pears. For the holidays, I ring them with an evergreen wreath and fill them with brightly colored tree ornaments. In the spring, I build a still life inside the lantern with a tiny piece of artwork and a bird's nest. In summer, I fill the lantern with limes or seashells.

I have a warm place in my heart for candles because I am convinced that both my house and I look our best when bathed in their soft and forgiving glow. When I entertain, I use a truckload of votives inside and out. Similarly, I go gaga over hanging glass votive cups suspended by thin wires. You'll find me on a ladder hanging votives from just about everything, like the trees in my garden and the dining room chandelier.

I also use a plethora of candlesticks in my daily decorating. Ornate silver candelabra are fixtures in my dining room. But instead of always filling them with taper candles, I often take an offbeat approach. I may top them with woodsy birch bark candles. Or, I might do something completely off-the-wall, like put candles on every arm of the candelabrum except one, topping the last arm with something unexpected.

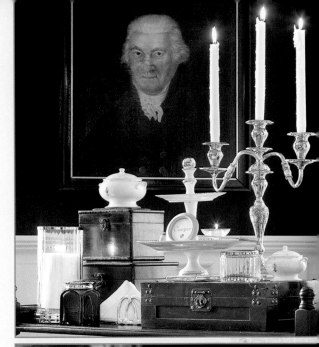

Mirrors and Glass

If you wander through the rooms of my home, you'll find mirrors in all shapes and sizes lending sparkle and shine to my interior decor. These timeless pieces have graced the walls of homes for centuries because they are affordable, attractive, and versatile.

The secret to their success is that mirrors look wonderful with everything you put near them. You'll never have to worry about a mirror clashing with your sofa upholstery or fighting the color of your walls.

Don't forget to use mirrors as backdrops for tabletop tableaux, chargers on your dining table, platters on your buffet, and trays on top of your upholstered ottoman.

Sleek and stylish and oh-so-accommodating, glass accents go anywhere and with anything in your home. I adore glass in every color and form conceivable, but cool, crisp, clear glass is my hands-down favorite.

Cut-crystal candy dishes, garlands of prisms, decanters with multifaceted lids, delicate stemware—I love them all in my decorating. Group glass accents by east windows where they can glow with the morning light. Or, combine these delicate beauties with heavy, dark, gritty accents to achieve that mixed-up balance that's at the heart of the Nell Hill's style.

Clear glass cloches, apothecary jars, compotes, and hurricanes have the magical ability to both contain and expose the items placed within them. Right now, two graceful apothecary jars hold court on my kitchen counter, one filled with puppy chow for Sister and the other with cat chow for Boots. If you like to freshen your home decor with seasonal accents, display the treasures of the season, like fresh fruits, under a glass cloche, on a glass cake stand, or in a glass hurricane.

Silver

I have been having a hot and heavy love affair with this high-voltage precious metal for years. Whether it's costly sterling silver, worn silver plate, or durable hotel silver, I love it all and use it in every room.

For me, silver dishes are both beautiful pieces of art and hardworking decorating tools. You'll never find my silver wrapped up, stored far from the light of day in a china closet. Instead, it is out earning its keep, bringing style and sophistication to displays all over my home. In my kitchen, old pieces of hotel silver decorate my cooktop. In my living room, a huge silver tray serves as a base for a constantly changing display. In my office, a silver cup holds my supplies.

If you have stacks of silver hidden away in your china cabinet, by all means, pull it out, give it a shine, and use it anywhere you want to add a bit of high style. A silver tray makes a great backdrop for a display in a dark bookcase. Silver vases look darling filled with toiletries. Silver bowls and baskets make great catchalls, holding your car keys and cell phone.

Since I prefer silver polished to a high luster, I try to give all my pieces a good polish every six months. But if I fall behind on my cleaning duties, it's not a crisis. I've found that silver with a recessed pattern looks better when it is slightly tarnished.

If you love the look of silver but are terrified by its upkeep, check out the beautiful aluminum serving pieces that are so popular today. The have the cool sparkle of silver but never need to be polished.

Books, Baskets, and Boxes

I'm always in trouble with Dan because I steal his books to use as props and pedestals all over our home. In my own defense, I don't have a choice. Dan buys so many, every open inch of floor space is overflowing with a tower of tomes.

Books make fabulous decorating tools because they give visitors a glimpse into a homeowner's interests and passions. I also love the physical properties of books old and new. Aged volumes, with their yellowed pages, beautiful illustrations, and soft leather covers, bring character and texture to displays. And coffee-table books work wonderfully as risers in still-life displays.

For fun, I'll select volumes whose subject matter complements or contrasts the items displayed around them. For instance, I might perch a bird's nest on top of a field guide or topiary next to a gardening book.

When I was just starting out in my career and had to decide whether to spend my meager paycheck on groceries or accessories for my apartment, I went for the home furnishings every time. And at the top of my list were versatile, beautiful, and affordable baskets. The same is still true today, but now, in additional to baskets, I'd also gladly blow my budget on antique wood boxes.

Aged wooden boxes have a story to tell, and I can't help but look at them and wonder where they've been and what they've seen.

I pick baskets for their color and shape, then put them to work everywhere. You'll find our cache of wine in an antique wicker basket tucked under my dining room buffet. In my foyer, I placed a trunk basket under my spindly legged console table to give the delicate table much-needed heft. Then I stuffed the basket full of extra blankets. In my bathroom, I use an iron basket to store toilet paper.

Botanicals and Natural Elements

I love to weave the brilliance of botanicals into my home decor, whether it's boughs of spring blooms in an urn, twisting vines laden with fall gourds on my buffet, or rosemary topiary on my kitchen windowsill. But as a notorious brown thumb, I've had a great deal of trouble keeping any type of flora alive in my home.

So, I was absolutely thrilled to find botanicals at the national home furnishings market that were every bit as beautiful as the real thing.

For spring decorating, I put a pot of artificial forced paper whites on my table or fill an ironstone pitcher with arms of silk forsythia. Summer finds a row of delicate topiary marching down the center of my dining room table. In fall, I fill baskets with vines and gourds, foliage, and berries. And when I decorate for winter, I deck the halls with yards of fabulous fake greens.

Many of my favorite decorative accents are from the wilds of nature. I love to bring untamed things from outside into my home, working them into displays with some of my most refined pieces. For instance, I hang deer horns and game trophies next to fine art. You'll find figurines of wild animals like stags and pheasant displayed on my dining room table. And no matter where you turn in my house, you're likely to find fruit, nuts, shells, and pebbles. I'm crazy about sheet moss and use it to top candlesticks, and I've even used it as a tablecloth!

But perhaps the accents that truly make my heart take flight are birds and their nests. Bird figurines in silver, iron, and glass are perched all sorts of places in my home. I put birds' nests under bell jars, in apothecary jars, atop the arms of candelabra, and nestled into the branches of floral arrangements.

Acknowledgments

I WANT TO THANK all of the people who worked extra hard to make this book possible, especially Micki Chestnut, who is so talented at crafting words and is able to channel my energy into pages of copy. I appreciate the contributions of the homeowners who made this book possible, not only for their generosity in opening up their homes and kitchens to us, but also for their willingness to do anything to make this book a success. Thanks to Lisa and Jon Cook and their darling girls, Ellie, Annabelle, and Georgia; Cynthia and Tom Hoenig; and Jean and Denny Lowe. I am so grateful to all of you. I also want to acknowledge Kathy Fernholz, for her help behind the scenes (and her sewing skills), and Kelly Acock at the Monarch Flower Company.

Thank you to the people at Andrews McMeel Publishing: Hugh Andrews, Kirsty Melville, and my editor, Dorothy O'Brien, for her careful oversight of this project. We couldn't have done it without her and the great and talented staff in the book group, including Julie Barnes, Diane Marsh, Caty Neis, Lesa Reifschneider, Julie Roberts, and Michelle Daniel. A special thank-you to the great promotion and publicity team there: Jennifer Collet, who goes to great lengths to help with promoting the book, along with Kathy

Hilliard and Special Sales associate Judi Marshall, for taking such good care of special sales efforts. Thanks again to Kathy Viele for the book club promotion.

None of this would be possible without my dedicated, faithful store employees, whose contributions to making Nell Hill's successful are immeasurable. I am so grateful to them for their help and talent. They are Melinda Allaman, Janelle Allan, Kathleen Armstrong, Glenna Batchelder, Jenny Bell, George Bilimek, Heather Brown, Carolyn Campbell, Ethel Campbell, Joan Carpenter, Heather Clark, Shirley Cline, Joyce Colman, Debbie Cooney, Joe Domann, Pam Dunn, Amanda Gonzalez, Brenda Graves, Judy Green, Amy Hale, Carol Hale, Gail Hansen, Angela Harris-Spurlock, Vicki Hinde, Kim Hobbs, Cynthia Hoenig, Dillon Kinsman, Mary Kuckelman, Pat Kuckelman, Nicky Liggett, Doe Loftus, June Lynn, Amy Minnis, Shannon Mize, Michelle Moccia, Gloria Nash, Lois Niemann, Andrew Nolting, Simon Nolting, Kenneth Otte, Cheryl Owens, Heather Owens, Donna Pierson, Lanie Schaeffer, Roxann Schied, Alice Scott, Kathy Sledd, Angie Stuebs, Gretchen Sullivan, Sarah Tucker, Tona Vanschoiack, Virginia Voelker, Autumn Werner, Lana White, Macy White, Cyreesa Windsor, and Kay Wolfe.

Special thanks are also in order to JoAnne Baker, Chubby Darrenkamp, Jo Hines, Arty Long, Lara Nomokomov, Cecelia Pellettiere, Geraldine Weishaar, and Marcelline Weishaar.

I am blessed with dear friends who are always there for me. Many of them are acknowledged above, but the following people know how much I count on them: Kim Amick, Marsee Bates, Gloria Case, Lynda Coulter, Melinda DiCarlo, Deann Dunn, Cheryl Hartell, Dianne Howard, Ann Humphreys, Melanie Krumbholz, Mary Lu Lotis, Darcy Mendenhall, and Nancy Neary.

And, always, thank you to my dear customers who keep coming back—I love you all!